SECRET BEHIND 4 WALLS

SCARLETT MINO IVY

Independently Published by Amazon

ISBN: 9781070709369

Copyright © 2019 Scarlett Mino Ivy

Cover Photo © 2019 Marvis Ramirez

All rights are reserved. No part of this book may be reproduced, scanned, or distributed in printed or electronic form without the author's permission.

Disclaimer: There are some poems with triggers in them, if you have been bullied, raped, tried to commit suicide, struggle with depression or have been racially discriminated/ profiled and do not what to be triggered please read with caution as some may trigger memories or dark thoughts. Also, some of these poems are personal and other are not about me but more of what I have learned from others.

DEDICATION

To my beloved little brother Christopher; when we were younger, I wasn't always the best sister and we didn't get along very well. As we grew up, we grew closer and now we are the best of friends, thank you for being my number one supporter in my life and for being my best friend I could never ask for a better little brother.

To my fiancé, Rolando; I love you with all my heart, we had a rough start, but things have been better as the years have gone by. you are the reason I am here today, thank you for accepting who I am.

And finally, to my mentor and friend DeAsia N.L. Zellner for believing in my writing and pushing me to continue with my writing. I gave up on my writing a while ago when my dreams were crushed, and you gave me so much hope to the possibilities of my writing career.

CONTENTS

True Me	1
Fake Smile	3
Oblivion	5
Amnesia	7
Ache	9
Fuck Up	13
Misunderstood	15
Misguided	17
Thoughts	19
Can You See	21
He Shouldn't Have Died	25
Planned Death	27
Insomnia	29
Depression	31
How Many Will We Let Go?	35
Are You There For Me?	39
Hidden	41
Mask	43
Lies through Smiles	45
Midnight Thoughts	47
I Ain't Scared of Dying	49
A Battle Everyday	51
Lies Behind the Walls	55
Pretty Picture	59
Afterlife	61
Not Alone	63
Suicide	65
Tired	67
Love at First Sight	69
Difficult to Open, Easy to Love	71
Fallen Angel (Part 1)	73

Fallen Angel (Part 2)	75
Demon in White (Sequel of Fallen Angel; Part 1)	77
Demon in White (Part 2)	79
Demon in White (Part 3)	81
Passion	85
Sex in the City	89
Forever 's a Promise	93
Love Letter	95
About the Author	99

TRUE ME

I was alone
No one by my side
Darkness was my best friend
And I wasn't in denial
I was mentally fucked up
I get it...
I was crazy
Would talk to the demons on my head
As if they were on my bed
And no, I wasn't always
crazy
This is how I came to be
When everyone around me
Always seemed to play me
So, I broke down and I stayed there
Not wanting to move or budge
So, I continued to be in my dark hole

Alone as always
Consumed by my thoughts and demons
That always fought
Now I sit her in bed
With these words in my head
Because I went insane
And now all the words I speak
Sound drained
So yes
I'm insane
There is nothing left I can say
Other than, thank you
Because now I know the true me

FAKE SMILE

I woke up every morning
Looking out my window
Cars passing by and I have this sort of
    smile
But the smile is all a lie
I smile to keep the truth inside
Late at night
No cars in sight
Pills on the floor
Blood near the door
Razor on my bed
Words in my head
The scars on my wrist will never fade
The hate in my heart will never sway
The tears in my eyes won't subside
I crossed my heart and hoped to die

I bury my sins that Father Almighty
Cleanse my soul
For all the wrong that I've done,
And I know that people had it worse then I
But that doesn't mean I wouldn't say goodbye
Bullies, surround me
I am lost can't you see
I am fighting this battle alone poor me
I cry at night hoping for love
That you will understand me
Let me be guided by your words
But all I do is fall
My heart is shattered
My soul is black
I can't do this anymore
Too much stress
Too much depression
I will never learn this lifelong lesson
To escape is to coward
To be free is to never win
But what's to be true from this fake smile

OBLIVION

I have a fear
I fear the oblivion
I fear the unknown
I fear the future
Now don't confuse this fear with every
*   other fear*
Like arachnophobia or aqua phobia
This fear is what I was born with
I didn't go through a traumatic
*   experience to fear the oblivion*
I came to fear it
I hate not knowing what will happen
I hate waiting for me to die or continue
*   living*
I want to know when I will find love
When I will have my heart broken

When I will struggle in my life
When I will rise to challenges in life
That way, I am ready
So yes,
I fear the oblivion
Because the oblivion fears itself

AMNESIA

I wish I forget
All that has happened
I wish I could never remember
All that was taught to me
As if I had
amnesia, I want to
forget
All the pain endured
All the hate that has rotten my heart
All the fights that have turned my
  body numb
Everything that has ever led me to
  become the way I am today
I wish I had Amnesia

ACHE

I sit here in pain, not physically
But mentally and emotionally
I ache for no pain
But I want the truth too much
Wishing I could free myself afterwards

It seems that the struggle
Is always here with me
And I wouldn't be here now
If guilt would leave me be
In peace instead of agony

I know there's many
Who had it worse than I
But that doesn't mean
I wouldn't say goodbye

People say I have a lot going for me
I am sorry, but I just can't see
I can't see because my worst enemy
Is not in my life
But me...

Cluttered minds
Cluttered thinking
It's hard to keep in touch
With what is happening around me
And not to worry too much

I feel that everybody is superior than me
And that I can't do anything right
This is how I felt my whole damn life
It didn't start last night

No confidence
No self-esteem
Everybody else is right
To speak my mind is to be a fool
A human that lacks intelligence
So, I try to just "sit tight and enjoy
    the ride"

I hope and pray that Jesus
The lord and savior will forgive me
To show pity is a disgrace

Afraid because I can't handle the truth

I always want to be right
But it only leads me to my failures and
    mistakes
I do all this because of
Fear
Power
Hate
And Judgement
Towards me

I want to be free from myself
From the world itself
To feel that I have a sense of humanity
Left inside of me
Instead,
Of a beast wanting to come out with rage

FUCK UP

Hello, I am a fuck up
No I am not lying
I really am
And I will explain how
I have a lack of expression
I can't seem to tell the people I love, that
    I love them
Nor can I seem to show them
I can't communicate very well
My feelings seem to bottle up in my
    throat
And when I finally open up
It shoots out like vomit never making
    sense and in random places
I can't seem to put my words together

Fuck Up

Making it complicated to answer even
*   the simplest of questions*
I don't have common sense
When someone says stop, I just go
And when someone says Yes, I hear No
Maybe it's because I am too scared to get
*   it wrong*
Or maybe I am just making sure I don't
*   do anything wrong*
But that never seems to go as planned
My depression gets in the way of my
*   thoughts and then I am left alone with*
*   these feelings of regret and despair*
So, I am a fuck up
And I am good at that then I ever was at
*   being perfect*

MISUNDERSTOOD

I seem to be misunderstood
In a way that doesn't seem to make sense
My words feel like air to those around me
My voice can't be heard but only felt
What I say can never make sense to the
    listener
Probably the reason I write
Because maybe if you can't hear me
You can at least read me
So, what I say doesn't make sense to
you Or maybe I am just too complex for
you Maybe my thoughts are higher than
you
    thought
And I make you think differently then you
    thought you did

*So, it doesn't make sense you say
Since my words feel so
meaningless, I guess I'm just
misunderstood*

*Because all I get is nonsense back
From those I wish had understood me*

MISGUIDED

I once believed in a God
I once believed that I had a protector
That I had a savior and an angel
I once thought my sins would be forgiven
Thought that I would be in Heaven when
    I die
But as I grow up
The less I believe in a God
The more I believe that things happen
    for a reason
But not by a God
The more I believe that my life wasn't
    God's plan
But my mom's error of not planning me
The more I believe my purpose to live is
    based from my actions

Not what God planed for me
I started to believe that God was just an imagination
A philosophy that someone made and called it a religion
Just to calm people's nerves and answer their existential questions
Oh, what will happen after
death? Where will we go?
Who will be there?
Etcetera
But no one really knows
And so we are all misguided
Built of philosophy's and ideologies that we don't even know if they are true
So, who is really naive?
Are we all misguided because of society?

THOUGHTS

*I can hear every word you spoke in
   my head
Like a fresh page in a book
I can remember you actions that hurt me
   emotionally
Like if your actions had marked my body
   of your sins
I can remember the hate in your eyes that
   shamed my every word
I can remember the judgement in your
   words as you spoke to me in tongues
   that pierced my skin
I can remember everything that you
   inflicted on me because all I can ever
   do is think
Thoughts is what clutters my mind*

Makes me feel like I have a clue to
    my life
Make me feel like I'm not alone
But that's the problem
My thoughts
All my thoughts have done is hurt me
Make me over analyze
And hurt my mind, body and spirit
So I will stop thinking
For the sake of my sanity

CAN YOU SEE

*Can you see me, when I call your name
When I hope for your forgiveness, when I
    cry for your love and care*

*Can you see me, when I grieve for
    my losses?
When I try to keep going for you, when I
    try to find you in my heart*

Can't you see me

*That I am suffering beyond belief falling
    into a hole of despair and hate*

Can you see me,

When I am falling and can't get up -more like- I don't want to
When I crawl away from my fears, cowering in the shadows of depression, when I feel worthless in my own head

Can you see me,
When I am trapped in my own thoughts
The thoughts that drag me into my demon's arms
When I am conflicted with my feelings

But do I have anything left?
When I cry myself to sleep, falling into my endless suicide attempts
Feeling like I failed, hurting every day since the day I realized my self-worth was as worthless as a pebble

Can you see me

When I am too hurt to even know what I am feeling that I am feeling that I am deceiving myself to the unknown, the oblivion
That I am done living, that I want to die

*To be free from the darkness in my head,
    to free myself from my own demons*

Can't you see me?

Because neither can I...

*But I was the girl that tricked my mind to
    think;
I was more alone than I really was....*

HE SHOULDN'T HAVE DIED

That man right there he shouldn't
    have died
He had a kind heart and a bright smile
That man right there he shouldn't
    have died
He had a beautiful little princess and a
    family
That man right there he shouldn't
    have died
He was just starting to fix his life
That man right there he shouldn't have
    died because he was loved and
    cared for
He was an amazing friend
A fun father
A great brother, cousin etc.

That man right there shouldn't have died
It was not his mistake
He didn't die on his own
He died because of someone's stupidity
And now others have suffered
That man right there shouldn't have died
So I write this in my bed crying tears for
him to come back because I need him
back and I want him back
I will see him again
I promise
But sadly, it won't be for a long
time RIP Kevin
We dearly miss you
And may you live in peace
And rock on in heaven

PLANNED DEATH

I planned my death
With every little detail
With no mistakes

I planned my death
To be on New Year's Eve
To go out with a bang

I planned my death
To take place at 12am
To start the new year dead and lifeless

I planned my death
Because if I didn't
I would have to live a life
That I didn't want to

*So, I planned my
death As a Suicide
plan*

INSOMNIA

Another sleepless night
Another cold night
All alone
In the dark
Everything is still
Everything is quiet
Everyone's asleep
Except for you
So, you get bored
You don't know what to do
So you sit in bed think
Or try to listen to music to pass the time
But it doesn't seem to work
It only makes it worse
So now you are depressed in bed and
    can't seem to sleep

DEPRESSION

Days of endless struggle
More hopeful pills today
Trying to appear 'normal'
In some sort of way
It seems that the struggle
Is always here with me
And I wouldn't be here now
If guilt would leave me be
I know that there has been many
Who've has it worse than I
But that doesn't mean I
wouldn't say goodbye
People say I have a lot going for me
I'm sorry, but I just can't see
I can't see because my worst enemy

Depression

Is not my life, but inside of me
Always on a roller coaster
Not much consistency
I'm nothing if I'm not up or down
I'm nothing if I'm not 'me'
Very little energy
Wanting to stay in bed
Wishing to be enthusiastic
Instead of feeling like I'm made of
  lead
Wanting to be excited

Wanting to care for more
But when nothing makes sense
It's hard to go use in the poor
Cluttered minds, cluttered thinking
It's hard to keep in touch
With what is happening around me
And not to worry too much
I feel that everybody is better than me
And that I can't do anything right
This how I felt all my damn life
It didn't start last night
No confidence, no self-esteem
Everybody is right
To speak my mind is to be a fool
So I have to just 'sit-tight'

Depression

Anyone of these problems
Would be a heavy vice
But when you have them
Living seems like a roll of dice

HOW MANY WILL WE LET GO?

Travon Martian, shot
Johnathan Paul, dead in custody
Denzel Brow, shot
Donald Dontay, tased
Tamir Rice, shot
Bryan Overstreet, hit by a cop car
Sandra Bland, found dead in jail or
  committed suicide
All an accident not believable
One-third of blacks killed by police
  in 2015
Thirty-nine percent unarmed were
  identified as black
And sadly, only eight out of one-hundred
  one police officers are charged with
  racial crimes

Why, why, why
Why do we let this happen?
Why do we let this be the norm
Those people right there
They shouldn't have died
They had hoped and dreams
Families and friends
And they died for no reason
People lying on the floor
Blood a rustic color painting the
    pavement
Lives lost, people in grief
People are suffering
We need to fight back
Stand for ourselves
Be the voice for others
Fight for what's right
Don't give up on yourself
We want to be free
Not downgraded, not put down
All this hate
It scared me to realize we are losing
    valuable lives
Lives that could have made a difference
In the constitution, it states Freedom,
    Liberty, and the Pursuit of Happiness
Well where is our freedom
In the shadows of our houses

In the cracks between the streets
In the gutters of the subway station
No
It's in our hearts
Our souls
Now we must rise up, fight and win
This battle for justice
Because, How many more will we let go?

ARE YOU THERE FOR ME?

How can you stay up there and not
    help me?
Help me believe
Help me be happy
Help me be myself
But how can I be myself
If you are not by my
side.
 I mean...
I love you God
But do you love
me.
 I mean...
I know the Bible says
Deny me in front of thy friend
And I will deny thee in front of thy father
But when I talk 'bout you God I get

nothing

But a look, I mean...
Are you there for me God
God I bled for you
God I followed you
God I prayed for you
God I needed you
But where were you
All these doors aren't open
I feel hopeless I thought your light would make me feel bright, but your light has don't nothing but made me color blind
How can I keep going if you're not going with me?
Don't you see I can't breathe?
When the air around me suffocates me, drains me of my energy
I feel broken
What can I do, don't you hear me when I speak to you?
Why let me suffer when you know how it feels

HIDDEN

Headphones in my ears
Darkness in my eyes
Hopelessness on my heart
Nothing left inside
I have friends
People I associate with
People I call family
But they don't know me too well
I have a secret
And I've hid it very well
I am never happy because I can't ever smile
The smile they see
It's a smile of pain
Of regret
A cry for help

That only I can understand, I fake
the happiness for my sake And for
those I love
Because of people saw what I really was
They would be afraid of me
So now I'm hidden
Behind   everything
Hidden for my sake
And for yours

MASK

Your smile is so beautiful
You laugh is charismatic
You look so happy
You make everything around your bright
You are confident in yourself
You're so reassuring to
people
You are gracious
You are perfect
You are unbreakable
You are happy
You are carefree
You are wonderful
You are everything
That's you can never be
This mask I have on
Is a persona I made

Someone that everyone thinks is perfect
Just to hide my inner demons
This person I made
Is wonderful
An image so amazing
No one can see her fall
But this mask has done nothing
But fool everyone
To make them believe I was happy
That's there was nothing wrong
So now this mask
Is a part of me
This mask
Is a curse

LIES THROUGH SMILES

Hi, I say, I missed you
I actually mean
Oh hay, I loved you, but you betrayed me

I'm fine, I'm just tired
I actually mean
I am not okay, I am tired of life, but you
    won't let me go

Oh those? My dog scratched me
I actually mean
I cut myself every night, but
    you never knew

Something is in my eye
I actually mean

*Yes, I am crying but you don't care so
    why should I bother?*

*I just love being alone
I actually mean
I hate being alone, but no one cares to be
    with me since no one loves me*

All these lies through one smile

MIDNIGHT THOUGHTS

The clock strikes 12am
And I'm still up
With my midnight thoughts
This little head has so much capacity
Ask me if I'm free
Insane I am
Can't you see
I'm losing my mind
With these thoughts
It's killing me
Honestly
Like can you find peace
With all the racket in my head
All alone in my bed
Feeling like a piece of lead
So I tell you

Midnight Thoughts

I can't sleep
I can't eat
I can't breathe right
Or think straight
Because of my thoughts
That clutter my mind
Give me anxiety
And it's so depressing
So now I'm up at 12am
With my midnight thoughts

I AIN'T SCARED OF DYING

In the darkest parts of my mind
I think of the worst ways to die possible
I could shoot my head into millions of pieces
I could tie a rope around my neck and fall
I could jump off the roof and fly down
I could pop pills till my mouth foams
And much more
But with each death I think about
The more excited I am
See I love the thought of death
How everything can end in a split second,

But I fear one thing
I'm scared of life

See when I am living, I feel like I can't breathe
The air around me suffocates me into an abyss
I am numb to everything and anything
And my body is just moving with the motions
Everything seems terrible while I am living
So, I'm not scared of dying
Because death would be great right now, I mean who would want to face reality It's too cruel
Being a dreamer was so much better
Yeah ignorance is the death of us
But if I had to be ignorant to be happy then shit, I'd do it
Maybe I am talking out my jaw
But death isn't so bad when you feel like you're dying already

A BATTLE EVERYDAY

About 100 years ago
Our brothers and sisters were enslaved
Our bodies used only to make them
    happy
To fit their needs
Our brothers cried out in anger
Our sisters wept in fear
Everything was dull at one point
Our women would be raped, and our
    men would be killed
But we fought
We never gave up
After years went by, time changed, and we
    got "rights"
It wasn't enough but it was progress
Right?

*Progress was the word they used to
    justify their actions
But compared to before
It seemed more than what we could
    afford
They let go of our brethren
We gained citizenship and the rights
    to vote
Then out came a speech
Martin Luther King had a dream
And to synthesize it he wanted equality
    and rights for all
Now I am sad to say we haven't gotten
    there yet
In the constitution, it states Freedom,
    Liberty, and the Pursuit of Happiness
Well where is our freedom
In the shadows of our houses
In the cracks between the streets
In the gutters of the subway station
No
It's within us
So, in order to make this change we must
    change us
Through an exchange in power
Through the destruction of ignorance in
    our minds that captivities one's self
We need to let it be known that*

*Although we have different pigments in
    our bodies, we all have the same fire
    in our souls, the same love on our
    hearts, the same passion in our minds*
So do not give up
Don't walk away
It's in our hearts
Our souls
*Now we must rise, fight and win this
    battle everyday*

LIES BEHIND THE WALLS

I once had an uncle
And oh, he was so sweet
Gave me love and treats
Pampered me well and I couldn't tell
The demons lurking inside of him
In his eyes
Late at night
Was a need for satisfaction
Oh! That need of satisfaction
Killed my soul...
See when I was 8 years old
I was told that my body was a gem
That no one should glance nor touch my flower
Oh! What a flower I was and oh! What pain was felt from my flower

See late one night
My uncle came to tuck me into bed
When mommy and daddy weren't home
And you see...
His eyes grew red and his face
    turned dark
And his voice went low and he changed.
He came close to me
Whispered good night
And as I slowly drifted to bed,
I felt his hands coil in my hair
His breathe hot on my neck
His... on my body
And I screamed but it was so silent when
    I scream
See he knew I would scream,
And he closed my mouth shut
And he ripped my clothes
He bruised my body
He hurt me so much
And I felt different,
I passed out on the bed while he took
    what wasn't his to take
And when I awoke my mom was next to
    me cleaning me up
Telling that I had my period that I was in
    women hood now

And all I did was smile and say
   sorry mom
I love you

When I was 21 my friend took me out to
   dinner
And we had so nice fun there were some
   laughs and chuckles
Everything seemed to go well
Dinner ended at 8 and I was tipsy
Had a couple to many drink
You insisted to take me home
Not knowing your plan was to hurt me
But I was too tipsy to argue
So, I got into your car
You drove to my place and I tried to leave
   the car
You locked the door
Asked if you can come up for a while
Told you no I was tired and I needed my rest
But you couldn't take no as an answer
You couldn't let my body say no to you
So you grabbed my wrists
Asked me again
I told you no more aggressively
That still didn't get through your head
You grabbed at my body

Violated my body and its rights
Told me to be quiet
You wouldn't stop
You wouldn't let go
I just cried and fought for the
  second time
By the end of it I was left with nothing
  but marks
Bruises and cuts for your wrongdoing
You kicked me out the car and I went in
  my house
Feeling different once more I
cried, I was raped again, and I
hated
  myself more
But all I did was look up at the sky and
  say sorry mom I love you.

PRETTY PICTURE

*I paint a pretty
picture, But the plot
has a twist
This pretty picture is on my wrist*

*My wrist is my canvas
And my blood is the paint*

*I draw a pretty picture
But there is a twist
For the pretty picture is on my arm*

*The scars won't
fade,
And neither will I So
deal with it bitch
Before I die*

*I color a pretty picture
But there is a twist.
Since this pretty picture is on my thighs*

*I cut in to deep
Not deep enough to die
But deep enough to feel the pain*

*I trace a pretty picture
But there is a twist
For the pretty picture is on my stomach*

*My friends called them stretch marks
Said they were beautiful because they
 were my own
I agreed
Just to keep my secret safe*

*I cut too much
And now too hard, too deep
I fall to the floor, bleeding
Blood everywhere
It was too late for your support*

*There was a pretty picture on my body
Now it's gone
And so am I*

AFTERLIFE

Closed eyes
Dark room
No light
Your colorblind
Silence surrounds
Everything is bleak
Your dead
There is nothing left
You won't see your family again
You won't see the world again
It's all gone

Or maybe there is
You get lifted up
Your wings spread and you fly
You see white

You see the light
You see your lost and forgotten family
You see a new world ahead

Or maybe it's something else
You get reborn
Brought back in a different life
With different family
Memories from your last past are faded
    and you can't seem to remember
You see all colors
You see light and dark
You feel new experiences with old
    knowledge
You see the world again

Whatever you believe
It's an afterlife

NOT ALONE

You sit in your room
All alone you are
Crying about life
Being too hard

You cry and you scream
Yet no one can hear you
Feeling so worthless
Even when people are with you

You look in the mirror
And you see yourself,
But no one can see
All the pain behind your eyes

As you look in the mirror

You realize something funny
You see someone behind you
That isn't with you

You turn around
And they are gone again
And you think about what that means

Then you realize
It was all a lie
You're not alone
You have people that care

So, wipe your eyes
Of the tears of shame

So, pick yourself up
Don't let yourself rot
Because you are not alone
As long as you have
Your heart of gold

SUICIDE

Suicide isn't the answer
I know we all heard that before
But this is coming for a person that attempted it herself
Suicide isn't the answer
It a coward way to escape a harsh reality
A way of telling life it was too hard
And you were too weak to fight back
Suicide isn't the answer
Because you could have had the bright future
Even if you didn't have the greatest childhood
And no this isn't aggression towards suicide
Because that makes me a hypocrite

But don't do it.
And I want to remind you
This isn't supposed to be a guilt trip
Because to say someone needs to stay for other people
Is malarkey
I mean, someone should want to live for themselves
Their own happiness
For their own life
Not someone else's
So
Always remember
That
Suicide
Isn't
The
Answer

TIRED

I am tired.
Of the constant reminders that I'm not
   good enough
Of the complaints you make based from
   my actions
Of the judgement that you scar and
   bruise upon my body to limit my self-
   worth
Of the fights that continue to go back and
   forth but will always become
   your way
Of the lash outs on me because you
   disagree with my opinions
Of the regret and pain, you have
   caused me

Tired

*Of the words that were turned to knifes
  that impaled through my fragile body
Of the cuts and scrapes that have been
  marked by your actions that have
  been done unto me
Of the hate that has consumed your heart
  and has poisoned mine
Of the screams and cried of your agony
  that have crippled my emotions
Of the mental insatiability that you gave
  me by making me feel like the enemy
I am tired of it all and now I don't know
  how to fix it...*

LOVE AT FIRST SIGHT

Two broken hearts
One soul
No house
But a home
Found peace
In a hopeless place
Found each other
Through the darkest days
No hope
Not faith
Thought life
Was a disgrace
Found each other
In the light of life

Fell in love
By first sight
Flames began to ignite
All hope regained
Love was found
Because it was love at first sight

DIFFICULT TO OPEN, EASY TO LOVE

Met you on a gloomy day
Felt all sad wasn't feeling gay
Sat alone with no love
You sat alone not wanting a hug
You came to me
Talked about my beauty
Told me a lot about you
In a matter of minutes
We started to date
Wasn't that easy
Lot of bumps in the road
Thought it would be easy
Just to give up
Everything we made of each other
We had fights
Said I had problems to fix

*Said you were
broken,
And I took the blame
Fixed myself but I still haven't won
    the game
Trying to fix you
Is difficult
You have a hard time of
communicating
 A hard time of understanding me
A hard time of loving yourself
A hard time of doing things for yourself
But even if it's difficult to get you to
    open up
It's so easy to fall in love with you
And I do everyday*

FALLEN ANGEL (PART 1)

I spread my wings and flown high
High enough to reach the sky
High enough to touch the clouds
Had no worries, no doubts

I spread my wings and flown high
My family saw I had what it takes
Said I had so much grace
Not to waste it all in space

I spread my wings and flown high
High so my friend could glide
Along we all flown
Never cared what was on our minds

I spread my wings and flown high

Till I saw my friends fall
One by one
They all seemed to drop

They all started to give up
There was loss of hope and loss faith
Looking behind
As I saw their grime face

I stopped and I turned back
Went to their aid
Helped them become strong enough
Till they could fly again

Then they spread their wings and fly,
And I was all alone
A fallen angel that fell
Saving the ones she loved.

FALLEN ANGEL (PART 2)

I am an angel that fell from above
Trying to save the ones I love
And with this curse
I have grown
To never give myself the aid I deserved
So I sit in my pit
Not wanting to move a bit
A fallen angel
In disguise
Filled with fear
To let someone help her
But down came a demon
Dressed in white
Pure at heart
No harm in mind
Outstretched his hand

I took it by chance
To find my strength rebuild
As he became weaker
He said he won't stop
Till I spread my wings and flew
   once more
Said all he ever wanted was his fallen
   angel to fly once more
So, I took this
hope Held it close
As I still fight this war
With him by my side
I know that once more I will soar
High enough to touch the clouds
   once more
But this time I won't be alone
I'll have him by my side
As my guide
To a place no fallen angel and demon in
   white can go

DEMON IN WHITE (SEQUEL OF FALLEN ANGEL; PART 1)

Satan had his right-hand man and his left
Satan was never the kind of guy to keep
    his word
Said that he would never betray his
    people
Said he would do what is best for his men
But one day
Satan called for his right-hand man
The demon in black
Said look
As the demon in black looked over,
He saw the fallen angel weeping
Satan laughed and took pity on her
Said break her soul
Shatter her heart
And I won't relinquish you from hell

The demon in black looked at her
　　once more
And walked to her
And as he got closer, he become more
　　angry
Until she looked up
The demon never saw so much pain in a
　　fallen angel
Never saw the fear in her eyes
When he saw her gaze
His heart changed
And his suit turned white
Satan called him a coward and left him
　　with the fallen angel
Now the demon in white looked at her
　　and smiled
Reached his hand out
Wanted to take a chance on her
Wanted to see her fly again
With those broken wings
So that he can fly too with her
Into a place that no fallen angel or
　　demon in white can go to.

DEMON IN WHITE (PART 2)

This demon dressed in white
Helped an angel see the light
Helped a fallen angel fly one more
Just so he can see her smile one more
This demon dressed in white
Used up his energy
Gave his all to this fallen angel
This demon dressed in white made
    sacrifices
And sometimes turned his white suit
    turned red
And through it all
He did not let it show
He simply
Put up his walls to make sure
He wouldn't see him without his grace

So, this demon dressed in white
Hid his pain
Just to make sure he can see this fallen
  angel fly once more
To a place no fallen angel and demon in
  white can go

DEMON IN WHITE (PART 3)

There was a demon in white
Who saw the light
Who flew with the fallen angel
And saw better days

But then he fell
Into the shore
He didn't know how to swim
So he started sinking right in

He couldn't breathe
He started to drown
Everything turned dark
He thought he had died

But the fallen angel had noticed

And dove in the water
Knowing she couldn't fly much
With her wet wings

She grabbed him and flew as much as
   she could till, she reached the
   shoreline
She passed out on the shoreline
As he awoke, he saw her

Thinking she was dead
He tried to revive her
She awoke
And he grew easy

Thought he lost her for good
Which made him tense
 Now he realized
That she truly loved him

Which made him
happy, But it wasn't
enough You see
This demon in white
Didn't find the light
He looked at it and looked the other way

See this demon in white

Demon in White (Part 3)

Was so hurt
He hurt himself

See this demon in white isn't happy He
just pretends to for the fallen angel
And it works too

See this demon in white only wants one
  thing
And that's to die
But the reason he isn't do it
Is because of I

See I love my demon in white
And I can't bear to lose him
But that won't stop him From
what he wants

See I want my demon in white to live
I really do
But all I know
Is that this demon in white
Is lost for sure
And I am the reasons
He doesn't know where to go

PASSION

It's 11 o'clock at night
And it's just me and you
In a bed all alone
It's just me and you It
shines bright outside
So, we half closed the shade
Just enough to see each other's body
    shapes forming
As I stare at your body
Baby, shapes are forming
You come close to me
Now it's body and body heat
The air is stall but I still manage to
    breathe
You kiss my cheek
Then my neck

Now I have you between my legs
All this heat got me feeling you instead
Now you are licking my clit
My pussy is dripping
Got me feeling
Like I'm Niagara Falls baby
And I'm your victim
Look baby take it slow
Make me feel every inch of your vibe
Baby lets go
See you turned me on
Now we going to play
How much can this pussy give
So I go on top baby
Just how you like it
Suck the tip
And maybe ride it Now
I'm on your cock
It's hard and juicy in
me
Got me having orgasm after orgasm
Babe you killing me
And when you
done,
I'll take it
Then we lay up
Touching each other still
There is passion in the air
And baby it's how I feel

So now you know my every kink
What turns me on
Now you know baby
That you're my all
And like I said
There will always be
Passion in the air

SEX IN THE CITY

It's 4am
And the city still lives
Cars and trunks honking
At each other, it is
Bright outside
With the city lights
Stars hide in pitch darkness
While we make stars in our hearts, the
Curtains closed
But the city lights still shine through
Just body on body nothing new
Kissing me in my body
Make me shameless
Got me feeling
Careless
Like can I give you my all

If you give me your all
You nibble on my neck
And I nibble at your chest
Kiss on your lips
And you kiss on my thigh
Our body's fit well
Like puzzle pieces
Got me feeling a connection
Between me and you
Ooo baby
You got me feeling you
You tell me my body is perfect
It's just how you like it
You make me feel secure
Bout my body
Now it's 5am and the sun coming up
You are giving me the goods
And won't stop
You hear me screaming your name,
But it isn't from pain
See baby you took my heart
Now your taking my soul
With that juicy cock in me
Got me going crazy
But baby
Don't stop now
Just cum in me
Make me your wife

*And love me baby
It's sex in the city
All this for you
Cuz baby you earned
me,
So, you earned it too*

FOREVER 'S A PROMISE

People say
Love never lasts
It always fades away
It's given to people
That didn't care anyways
People say
Give up on love
Because it's never real
It's always made of steel
It hurts, forreal
People say
Loves a joke
It's for suckers and believers
But the you become victim
And your hurt from believing
But that's not true

Because I'll say this once
I fell in love with a boy who never
    thought he could be loved
And now I'm here
With his heart and soul
And I promise
That I'll love him forever

LOVE LETTER

Rolando,
This is my love letter to you
And I know you have read it all before
But there is more that I wish to express
    to you
See, I have a dream every night
That we will fly as high as a kite
Flying into the endless possibilities of
    our future
I wake up with a smile on my face
Feeling this happiness every day
The room seems to be brighter every day
And it's all because you're my one
    thought every morning
I text you a lot

Love Letter

*Just because I miss you and other time
    just to know your alive
I call you to hear your sexy voice
    sometimes just because I want to talk
I get home and look at the photos you
    gave me and smile
Look at the necklace and ring and kiss
    them both
All because I can never be able to
    appreciate you enough
See you are the light of my life
You are the apple of my eye
You have the key to my heart and soul
You are my everything
I want so much with you
I want to live with you when I'm 18 and
    cuddle at night
I want to go to college with you and get
    my certification from med school and
    you being a detective
I want to marry you at 22 and go on a
    honeymoon
I want to work in a hospital and be your
    personal doctors
I want to make money with you and
    save up
I want to get a house with you at 27*

*I want to have kids at 29 or whenever we
    are financially stable
I want to teach these kids with you
I want to see these kids grow with you
I want to grow old with you and die
    with you
I want everything with you
I love you
And every day I fall more in love
    with you
Every day I appreciate you more
Every day I want you more
Rolando
This love letter is for you
And only you
Because you are my husband, my
    soulmate, my forever boy, my
    everything
I love you
Through Thick and Thin
Through Bullet Wounds and Scars
Forever and Ever
1-29-18
I love you, Rolando
Sincerely, Your wife*

ABOUT THE AUTHOR

I am an 18-year old college freshman; Brooklyn born. I was raised from a Hispanic middle-class family. Growing up I was a little strange. My mind worked differently than anyone else's. I was always clueless on the most obvious thing and under- stood the darkest, deepest things. Now it may sound like you, but since I could remember I was bullied. I thought I was laughing with them instead of them laughing at me. But when I found out the truth, I started writing.

Poetry was my outlet and it saved me along, music was also my escape from reality. I wrote about deep topics; topics that people didn't discuss on a regular basis. See I wanted to be the voice that people didn't have. The voice that people didn't share or didn't want to share but have no doubt I will share them with you. I want to teach people and make people feel understood so please read my poetry with an open mind. My poetry is powerful, and no one knew because I was afraid to be judged but now, I don't care for the judgement and I want to share my writing.

For more information about the author: Instagram: scarlett_mino_ivy

Email: scarlettminoivy18@gmail.com

Snapchat: cutepopulargeek

Please follow the accounts and support her cause of making people aware of mental illness and struggles and to help people that do struggle feel understood.